"The best musical of 2017 . . . Exquisite . . . It kept evoking for me Anton Chekhov's plays set in Russian backwaters, where an interruption in the boring, isolating routine of the characters suddenly opens a window onto their common humanity . . . In the company of strangers, the characters begin to see themselves anew. The sacred honor of hospitality compels patience and presence, but it's music that ultimately dismantles barriers . . . At a time when politics is dividing us not only from each other but also from ourselves, *The Band's Visit* offers balm for the breach in our souls."

—CHARLES MCNULTY, *LOS ANGELES TIMES*

"'Beautiful' is a word we bandy about in the daily pursuit of adjectives to describe the things we love. But even in an entertainment world overrun with superlatives, this is the one you're compelled to use to describe *The Band's Visit* . . . It is gentle, soulful, tuneful—and the best new musical on Broadway."

—PETER MARKS, *WASHINGTON POST*

"An evening of enchantment . . . A uniquely unconventional musical told in a new manner."

—STEVEN SUSKIN, *HUFFINGTON POST*

"Overwhelmingly joyous . . . *The Band's Visit* takes place in the desert and, like a mirage, it shimmers. But better. Because this hushed, heart-melting musical is real—and truly magical . . . The show is a quiet musical meditation that casts a spell through its songs . . . Moses and Yazbek have created something rare, grown-up and special. The book packs warmth, wit and economy. Irresistible songs blend strains of Arabic and Israeli melodies and flecks of jazz . . . It works so wonderfully because it never overstates. It doesn't belt. It whispers. It doesn't grab. It reaches . . . it shines."

—JOE_____, *NEW YORK DAILY NEWS*

"An embraceable musical fable about the surprising friendships that bloom in the middle of a political desert . . . Connections are made on little things, everyday things, common things we all share . . . Broadway theatergoers looking for something off-the-beaten-musical-track should be charmed by this unassuming show. But this disarming musical has the emotional depth that holds up to repeated viewings and the offbeat charm that could make it a cult hit."

—MARILYN STASIO, *VARIETY*

"*The Band's Visit* is a sweet, haunting stopover in the desert . . . This is a play about waiting, and loneliness, and the human need to connect with another human . . . There are no elaborately choreographed dance sequences or dramatic betrayals or plot twists. The only revelation is that there are no revelations; that humans and their petty, internal concerns, their hopes and failures, are worthy enough to sing about . . . It's a quiet, beautiful thing *The Band's Visit* does."

—DANA SCHWARTZ, *ENTERTAINMENT WEEKLY*

"Beguiling music and lyrics by David Yazbek and a spare and shrewd book by Itamar Moses . . . In *The Band's Visit* we get the glorious nothingness of an uneventful night in the middle of nowhere . . . It is a show about nothing, but it fills the stage with feeling—the muted kind that dwells in missed connections."

—MICHAEL SCHULMAN, *NEW YORKER*

·THE·
BAND'S VISIT

·THE·
BAND'S VISIT

MUSIC AND LYRICS BY
DAVID YAZBEK

BOOK BY
ITAMAR MOSES

Based on the film by Eran Kolirin

THEATRE COMMUNICATIONS GROUP
NEW YORK
2018

The publication of *The Band's Visit* by David Yazbek and Itamar Moses, through TCG's Book Program, is made possible in part by the New York State Council on the Arts with the support of Governor Andrew Cuomo and the New York State Legislature.

TCG books are exclusively distributed to the book trade by Consortium Book Sales and Distribution.

Library of Congress Control Number: 2018015286
ISBN 978-1-55936-586-4 (trade paper) / ISBN 978-1-55936-901-5 (ebook)

A catalog record for this book is available from the Library of Congress.

Book design and composition by Lisa Govan
Cover photographs by Sophy Holland and Matthew Murphy, design by AKA

First Edition, May 2018

For my Father,
who showed me Lebanon.

—DY

For my Grandparents.

—IM

·THE·
BAND'S VISIT

The Band's Visit had its world premiere at Atlantic Theater Company (Neil Pepe, Artistic Director; Jeffory Lawson; Managing Director) in New York on November 11, 2016. It was directed by David Cromer. The scenic design was by Scott Pask, the costume design was by Sarah Laux, the lighting design was by Tyler Micoleau, the sound design was by Kenneth C. Goodwin, the choreography was by Patrick McCollum, the projection design was by Maya Ciarrocchi; the music director was Andrea Grody and the production stage manager was Richard A. Hodge. The cast was:

TEWFIQ	Tony Shalhoub
SIMON	Alok Tewari
HALED	Ari'el Stachel
CAMAL	George Abud
DINA	Katrina Lenk
ITZIK	John Cariani
PAPI	Daniel David Stewart
IRIS	Kristen Sieh
AVRUM	Andrew Polk
ZELGER	Bill Army
ANNA	Sharone Sayegh
JULIA	Rachel Prather
SAMMY	Jonathan Raviv
TELEPHONE GUY	Erik Liberman
OTHER BAND MEMBERS	Sam Sadigursky (reeds), Harvey Valdes (oud), Garo Yellin (cello)

The Band's Visit opened on Broadway at the Ethel Barrymore Theatre on November 9, 2017. The producers were Orin Wolf, StylesFour Productions, Evamere Entertainment, Atlantic Theater Company, David F. Schwartz, Barbara Broccoli, Frederick Zollo, Grove·REG, Lassen Blume Baldwin, Thomas Steven Perakos, Marc Platt, The Shubert Organization, The Baruch/Routh/Frankel/Viertel Group, Robert Cole, deRoy-Carr-Klausner, Federman-Moellenberg, FilmNation Entertainment, Roy Furman, FVSL Theatricals, Hendel-Karmazin, HoriPro Inc., IPN, Jam Theatricals, The John Gore Organization, Koenigsberg-Krauss, David Mirvish, James L. Nederlander, Al Nocciolino, Once Upon A Time Productions, Susan Rose, and Paul Shiverick; the executive producer was Allan Williams. The cast and creative team remained the same as the Atlantic Theater Company production, except Kai Harada was the sound designer, and there were the following cast changes and addition:

PAPI	Etai Benson
TELEPHONE GUY	Adam Kantor
OTHER BAND MEMBER	Ossama Farouk (darbuka)

Characters

The Band:

TEWFIQ, conductor of the Alexandria Ceremonial Police Orchestra

SIMON, assistant conductor and the clarinetist in the Alexandria Ceremonial Police Orchestra

HALED, the trumpet player in the Alexandria Ceremonial Police Orchestra

CAMAL, the violinist in the Alexandria Ceremonial Police Orchestra

OTHER BAND MEMBERS, reeds, oud, cello, and darbuka in the Alexandria Ceremonial Police Orchestra

The Townspeople:

DINA, a café owner in Bet Hatikvah

ITZIK, a young father

PAPI, an employee at Dina's café

IRIS, Itzik's wife

AVRUM, Iris's father

ZELGER, Papi's friend

ANNA, Zelger's girlfriend

JULIA, Anna's cousin

SAMMY, a married man

TELEPHONE GUY, a young man waiting at a telephone

Also:

SAMMY'S WIFE, TWO SOLDIERS, A TICKET GIRL, A SECURITY GUARD, A DJ

SETTING

Israeli, 1996.

An airport bus station; the town of Bet Hatikvah; the city of Petah Tikvah.

NOTES

The attempt with both Hebrew and Arabic has been to use contemporary, regionally appropriate dialect with the exception of the occasional use of classical Arabic, as in Tewfiq's song "Itgara'a." Arabic translations in the script are by Mouna R'miki. Hebrew translations are by Zohar Tirosh-Polk and Jonathan Raviv. The author would also like to thank David Dryer, Ossama Farouk, and Sharone Sayegh for linguistic help along the way.

Mentions in the script of "Band Members" other than Tewfiq, Simon, Haled, and Camal generally refer to four nonspeaking roles played by onstage musicians—oud, reeds, cello, and darbuka (though when violin is also necessary, as for instance in "Haj-Butrus" or the "park" scene, they are joined either by Camal, if the actor performing the role can actually play violin, or an additional onstage violinist). As day becomes evening becomes night, the appearances of these musicians become increasingly fluid, ghostly, and nonliteral.

Songs

Overture	*The Band*
Waiting	*The Residents of Bet Hatikvah*
Welcome to Nowhere	*Dina, Itzik, Papi*
It Is What It Is	*Dina*
The Beat of Your Heart	*Avrum, Itzik, Simon, Camal*
Soraya	*The Band*
Omar Sharif	*Dina*
Haj-Butrus	*The Band*
Papi Hears the Ocean	*Papi*
Haled's Song about Love	*Haled, Papi*
The Park	*The Band*
Itgara'a	*Tewfiq*
Something Different	*Tewfiq, Dina*
Itzik's Lullaby	*Itzik, Camal*
Something Different (Reprise)	*Dina*
Answer Me	*Telephone Guy, Ensemble*
The Concert	*The Band*

Scene 1

Overture begins. Then, projected: "Once not long ago a group of musicians came to Israel from Egypt." This vanishes. Then: "You probably didn't hear about it. It wasn't very important." Then the overture ends and we snap to:

An airport bus station. Tewfiq and the Band are standing in a line, their musical instruments and baggage around them. They have been waiting here a while. There's a ticket booth with a Ticket Girl inside. Two Female Soldiers in uniform walk past, with weapons. A moment. Then Tewfiq turns to Simon:

TEWFIQ: *Hooma el mefrood ya'abloona imta?* [When were they supposed to meet us?]

SIMON: *Kano el mafrood yekoono hena hidaashar we nuss—* [They were supposed to be here eleven-thirt—]

CAMAL (*Looking at the soldiers*): Maybe we should speak English.

SIMON: They were supposed to be here eleven-thirty.

(Haled turns to the Soliders. Tewfiq thinks he is perhaps going to ask for directions or advice but instead:)

9

HALED: Hello. I am Haled. I am musician.

SOLDIER 1: Okay.

HALED: Actually I play two instrument. *Rik* [tambourine] and trumpet. You know Chet Baker? (*Singing*) "My funny valentine—"

TEWFIQ: *Haled!*

(*Haled, annoyed, comes back into the line. A moment. Tewfiq looks at his watch. Then sighs. Then:*)

(*Definitively*) We will take the bus.

SIMON: What? But—

(*But Tewfiq is already turning to the Band:*)

TEWFIQ: *Intibah!* [Attention!] We are here to represent our country. And as always we will do so with the highest standard of both musicianship and professionalism. (*Off Haled's smirk*) There are those who doubt this. Unfortunately, some of those people are in control of our funding. So there will be no embarrassments. There will be no mistakes. Nothing to give our critics ammunition against us. (*To Simon*) Where are we going?

SIMON (*Reading from a slip of paper*): "Betah Tikvah."

(*Simon starts to go to the ticket booth, but then . . .*)

TEWFIQ: *Haled.*

HALED: What. (*Beat*) My English is not so good, maybe—

TEWFIQ: Go!

(*Haled sighs and goes toward the ticket booth.*)

CAMAL: And be on the lookout.

HALED: For what?

(*Camel gestures, "Isn't it obvious?" Haled shakes his head and goes to wait in line behind an Israeli. Then:*)

SIMON: By the way. I thought perhaps this trip could be my chance to conduct, in concert. If it's okay. I would need to rehearse, with the band—

TEWFIQ: Maybe next time.

(Haled has now reached the front of the line.)

TICKET GIRL: *Ken?* [Yes?]

HALED: Hello. May I have . . . You have . . . beautiful eyes.

TICKET GIRL: What?

HALED: Do you know Chet Baker? *(Singing)* "My funny valentine—"

TEWFIQ: *Haled!*

HALED *(Sighs. Then)*: We would like tickets to *Betah Tikvah.*

TICKET GIRL: *Petah Tikvah* or *Bet Hatikvah?*

(Haled looks to Tewfiq. Beat. Lights.)

SCENE 2

Music, as the town appears, in the dawn light, as if from a mirage. We are on the street outside Dina's café and also various living areas. Some distance away there is a telephone booth. Papi enters and begins opening the café.

PAPI:

> WAITING.
> WHAT'S NEW HERE?
> YOU'RE WAITING,
> I'M WAITING
> 'CAUSE THAT'S WHAT
> WE DO HERE,
> SAME AS WE DO EVERY DAY
>
> FOR SOMETHING,
> I DON'T KNOW,
> TO HAPPEN, YOU KNOW,
> JUST SOMETHING DIFFERENT
> TO HAPPEN.

> JUST WAITING
> FOR SOMETHING TO CHANGE,
> JUST A CHANGE . . .

(By now Avrum has appeared. He sings:)

AVRUM:

> SOMETIMES IT FEELS LIKE
> WE'RE MOVING IN A CIRCLE,
> AROUND AND AROUND WITH
> THE SAME SCENERY
> GOING BY
>
> BUT NO ONE'S COMPLAINING,
> WE'RE EXPERTS AT WAITING . . .

ENSEMBLE:

> OHHH . . .

(Lights up on Itzik and Iris's apartment. Itzik is on the couch. Iris comes home from work, tired, in a nurse's uniform. There is a crib in another room.)

ENSEMBLE:

> AHHHH . . .

ITZIK:

> TIME'S LIKE A RIVER SOMETIMES.
> TIME IS AN OCEAN.
> THIS SOFA IS MY BOAT
> AND I'M JUST DRIFTING RIGHT ALONG.

ITZIK:	IRIS:
TIME IS LIKE SYRUP	JUST WAITING FOR SOMETHING
AND I'M THE BUG STUCK IN THE SYRUP,	TO HAPPEN, FOR ANYTHING TO HAPPEN.
JUST KIND OF TRYING TO FIND OUT WHAT I'M DOING WRONG.	WAITING TO FIND OUT WHAT I'M DOING WRONG.

(Itzik approaches the café where Papi has finished setting up and joins him.)

ENSEMBLE:
>AHHH . . .

(Dina joins Papi and Itzik at the café.)

>AHHH . . .

DINA:
>YOU KNOW WHAT I THINK,
>THERE'S TWO KINDS OF WAITING—
>THERE'S THE KIND WHERE YOU'RE EXPECTING
>>SOMETHING
>NEW OR EVEN STRANGE,
>BUT THIS KIND OF WAITING,
>YOU KEEP LOOKING OFF OUT INTO THE DISTANCE
>EVEN THOUGH YOU KNOW THE VIEW IS NEVER
>>GONNA CHANGE.

D/P:	AV/J/IR:	Z/AN/T G:	IT:
YOU WAIT . . .	WAITING FOR		
	SOMETHING	FOR SOME-	
AND S:	FOR ANYTHING	THING	TIME IS
YOU WAIT . . .	TO HAPPEN	FOR ANYTHING	A RIVER
	JUST WAITING	TO HAPPEN	SOMETIMES
	FOR ANYTHING	I'M WAITING	TIME IS
	I'M WAITING		AN OCEAN

AND IR/Z:	AV/J:	AN/T G:	
YOU JUST WAIT	TO HAPPEN	WAITING FOR	I CAN'T CON-
	FOR	SOMETHING	TROL MY LIFE
	SOMETHING	TO HAPPEN	SO I'M JUST
	TO HAPPEN	JUST SOME-	DRIFTING
		THING	RIGHT ALONG.

15

	J:		
AND AN:	FOR ANYTHING	T G:	AND AV:
AND WAIT	TO HAPPEN	FOR SOME-	YOU WAIT . . .
	YOU WAIT	THING WAIT	

(And, just as Dina disappears back inside her café . . . the Band appears: Tewfiq, Simon, Haled, Camal and the other Musicians, in uniforms, dragging rolling suitcases. Papi and Itzik stare at them.)

TEWFIQ: Good afternoon.

(A moment. Papi turns to call inside the café:)

PAPI: Dina? A General is here to see you!

(Dina emerges from the café, bringing coffee to Itzik and Papi. Tewfiq freezes, for a moment, seeing her.)

DINA: Yes?

TEWFIQ: Good afternoon.

DINA: Good afternoon to you, too.

TEWFIQ: I wonder if you could be so kind as to direct us to Arab Cultural Center.

DINA: I'm sorry?

TEWFIQ: My apologies. I am Colonel Tewfiq Zakaria, commander of the Alexandria Ceremonial Police Orchestra. *(He gestures to the Band)* We have been invited by the local cultural department to play at the initiation ceremony of the Arab Culture Center here tomorrow. And, if you would be so kind as to direct us there, we would be most grateful.

(Tewfiq bows slightly. Dina and Itzik exchange an incredulous look. Then:)

ITZIK: *Where* are you from?

TEWFIQ: We are from Egypt.

ITZIK *(Wow!)*: Egypt!

TEWFIQ: Um. Yes.
DINA: And *who* invite you?

(*Tewfiq fumbles inside his jacket for some paperwork.*)

TEWFIQ: The Betah Tikvah Cultural Department.
ITZIK: Petah Tikvah? Or Bet Hatikvah?
TEWFIQ: Betah Tikvah.
ITZIK (*To Dina*): *Ani choshev sh'hoo rotseh et* Petach *Tikvah.*
    [I think he needs *Petah* Tikvah.]
DINA: Do you need Petah Tikvah?
TEWFIQ: Yes. Betah Tikvah.
DINA/ITZIK (*Variously*): No, not Bet Ha. Petah. Not Beh. Peh. Peh.
    Peh. Petah Tikvah.
DINA: There is not Arab Center here.
TEWFIQ: No Arab Culture Center?
ITZIK: No.
DINA: No. Not Arab culture, not Israeli. Not culture at all.

> LET ME TELL YOU ABOUT PETAH TIKVAH—
> SUCH A CITY, EVERYBODY LOVES IT.
> LOTS OF FUN, LOTS OF ART, LOTS OF CULTURE—
> THAT'S PETAH TIKVAH—
> WITH A "P."
> WHERE YOU ARE, THIS IS *NOT* PETAH TIKVAH.
> SUCH A CITY, NOBODY KNOWS IT.
> NOT A-FUN, NOT A-ART, NOT A-CULTURE.
> THIS IS BET HATIKVAH,
> WITH A "B"

ITZIK:

> LIKE IN BORING,

PAPI:

> LIKE IN BARREN,

ITZIK:

> LIKE IN BULLSHIT,

PAPI:

> LIKE IN BLAND.

DINA:

> LIKE IN BASICALLY BLEAK AND BEIGE AND
> BLAH, BLAH, BLAH . . .
>
> STICK A PIN IN A MAP OF THE DESERT,
> BUILD A ROAD TO THE MIDDLE OF THE DESERT,
> POUR CEMENT ON THE SPOT IN THE DESERT—
> THAT'S BET HATIKVAH.

DINA/ITZIK/PAPI:

> WELCOME TO NOWHERE.

(Eight-bar instrumental, in which first Itzik and then Papi spins a lazy susan on a table as though this is very entertaining. Then, over the next eight bars, Dina gives the following "inspiring" speech:)

DINA: Behold, where there was once only desert, the town of Bet Hatikvah. See! Apartments. Gaze upon! My café. While you're here, be sure to go back and forth between my café and the apartments! So much to explore!!!

PAPI:

> PICK A SAND HILL OF YOUR CHOOSIN',

ITZIK:

> TAKE SOME BRICKS THAT
> NO ONE'S USIN',

DINA:

> BUILD SOME BUILDINGS,
> PUT SOME JEWS IN,

DINA/ITZIK/PAPI:

> THEN BLAH BLAH BLAH

ITZIK:

BET HATIKVAH!

DINA/ITZIK/PAPI:

HERE YOU ARE IN RENOWNED BET HATIKVAH.
GO AHEAD LOOK AROUND BET HATIKVAH.
LUCKY YOU, YOU HAVE FOUND BET HATIKVAH.
WELCOME TO NOWHERE.

PAPI:

WITH A "B"!

DINA/ITZIK/PAPI:

WELCOME TO NOWHERE.

(A moment. Then Zelger walks past, with a boombox, blasting Israeli hip-hop. He checks out Tewfiq.)

ZELGER (Mockingly): Hey! General! (To himself) Wow.

(Zelger is gone. Tewfiq, struggling to maintain his dignity, turns, walks over to the Band and right up to Haled.)

TEWFIQ: Ya khreb beetuk! Shooft aamelt eeeh! [What's wrong with you! Look what you've done!]
HALED: Aamelt eelee inta ooltillee alee. [I did what you told me.]
TEWFIQ: Oultilek taguibna fee ilmaakan il'ghulit? [I told you to bring us to the wrong place?]
HALED: Inta oolt Bet Hatikvah. [You said Bet Hatikvah!]
TEWFIQ: Khalas! [Enough!] Your careless behavior has embarrassed us for the last time. And when we return to Alexandria you will be summarily expelled from the band fowran! [immediately!] (Generally) Yala! Yala! [Come on!]

(Tewfiq grabs his suitcase and starts wheeling away. The rest of the Band starts to follow, except for Haled, who, after a moment, says:)

HALED: *Ya'ani* [I mean], can we eat first?

(*Tewfiq stops. He slowly turns around. The rest of the Band starts to nod and murmur in agreement. A beat.*)

TEWFIQ: *Istaf-hum.* [Line them up.]
SIMON: *Yala!* [Come on!]

(*Tewfiq goes back over to the café as Simon corrects the Band's alignment.*)

DINA: Hello again.
TEWFIQ: Madam, I would like . . . on behalf of the Alexandria Ceremonial Police Orchestra. We should be grateful if you could be so kind to help us. In the light of the circumstances.
DINA: How can I help you?
TEWFIQ: Would it be possible to dine here?
DINA: It's a restaurant here?
TEWFIQ: Yes, but . . . You see we have little Israeli money left. We don't need something special. Just some bread. Something light.
DINA: I think we can fit you in.

(*Music, transition . . .*)

Scene 3

A short time later. The Band eats, awkwardly apart from Papi and Itzik, outside the café. Simon begins to play his clarinet. Haled plays backgammon with another Musician. Dina is inside, on the phone. Simon stops playing.

ITZIK: Why you stop?
SIMON: I didn't finish it.

(*Beat.*)

ITZIK: You *wrote* this?
SIMON: Yes. It is an overture for a concerto. But I didn't finish it.
ITZIK: It's nice.

(*Dina finishes her call inside and comes back out. She sits next to Tewfiq, who is sitting alone.*)

DINA: There is no more bus today.
TEWFIQ: No more bus?

DINA: Uh-uh. Finito.
TEWFIQ: Hotel?
DINA: Hotel? Here? No.
TEWFIQ: Of course.

(*Beat.*)

CAMAL: We should call the embassy.
TEWFIQ (*Quickly, shaking his head*): La. [No.]

(*Dina gathers that this is a real problem.*)

DINA: When is your show?
TEWFIQ: It is tomorrow evening.
DINA (*To Itzik*): *Tagid, Itzik. Ata yachol lakachat shlosha mehem?* [Say, Itzik. Can you take three of them?]
ITZIK: *Ma?* [What?]
DINA (*To Tewfiq*): You know what, General? You can stay here tonight with us if you want.
TEWFIQ: What, you mean here?
DINA: Yes. I can take some. Papi can make room here, in the restaurant. And Itzik can take some too.
ITZIK (*To Dina*): Hey! *Ma at omeret lo?* [What are you telling him?]
PAPI (*To Dina*): *Ani yotseh haerev!* [I'm going out tonight!]
DINA (*To Papi and Itzik*): *Ze beseder.* [It's okay.]
PAPI: *Aval—* [But—]
DINA: *Beseder!* [It's okay!] (*Back to Tewfiq*) And then tomorrow morning you take the bus.
TEWFIQ: No, you've . . . done too much already.
DINA: Okay. But really. I just want that you know that we here in Bet Hatikvah will be very honored to have the Alexandria Ceremonial Police Orchestra with us.
TEWFIQ: Really.
DINA: Really.
TEWFIQ: Your . . . husband will not mind?

(*Dina chuckles.*)

DINA: If I ever see him again I'll ask. *(Beat)* By the way, I'm Dina.
TEWFIQ: Tewfiq.

> *(Music, transition, during which the townspeople divide up the Band: Papi sets up several Band Members in the café. Itzik takes Simon and Camal off with him. Initially Haled attempts to go with them as well, but then Tewfiq insists Haled come with him, with Dina. Dina brings Tewfiq and Haled to her place and . . .)*

Scene 4

Lights up, discovering Dina leading Haled and Tewfiq into Dina's apartment. She gestures around herself as if to say, "This is it."

DINA: I don't have much food, drink. Not many visitors. Some coffee?

HALED: Yes, please.

TEWFIQ (*Simultaneously*): No, thank you, we are fine.

(A moment. Dina chuckles and goes to her kitchen area. She starts a coffee machine. During this, Haled goes to another door, presumably to her bedroom, and peeks in. Tewfiq glares at him. Haled steps back. Then:)

HALED: It's quiet here.

DINA: Dead.

(Dina turns on her radio. Music plays faintly.)

Alexandria is big city, yes? Lot of people, lights.

HALED: Noise.

DINA: It's good! You feel you live. It's not like here.

HALED: You don't like to be here?

DINA: It's my life. I got used to. But, you know, I used to be . . . dancer? And sometimes, I thought, if I move to a bigger city, I could maybe . . .

HALED: Why you don't?

(Dina takes out a watermelon and a knife.)

DINA:

> I WAS ROMANTIC
> AND YOUNG AND STUPID.
> I MET MY HUSBAND,
> YOU KNOW HOW THESE THINGS GO—

(She slices the watermelon extra hard.)

> YOU'VE GOT YOUR STORY,
> YOU'RE IN YOUR MOVIE,
> YOU ARE THE HERO,
> YOU THINK YOU KNOW.
>
> YOU THINK YOU KNOW WHAT HAPPENS.
> YOU THINK IT ALL WILL HAPPEN.
> YOU THINK IT ALL WILL GO.
> A CERTAIN WAY.

(She slices the watermelon some more.)

> YOU THINK YOU KNOW THE STORY,
> YOU THINK A HAPPY ENDING?
> BUT YOU DON'T KNOW THE STORY.

(Dina puts a plate of watermelon slices in front of them.)

> Here.

HALED: Do you like Chet Baker?

DINA: No. *(To Tewfiq)* What about you, General? You have someone waiting for you, in Egypt? A wife?

TEWFIQ: Me? No. I had, at one time, but . . .

DINA: Ah—

> BUT THEN YOU SEE IT,
> YOU LEARN YOUR LESSON,
> GROW UP A LITTLE,
> YOU SETTLE IN,
>
> THEN IT IS WHAT IT IS,
> YOU'VE GOT WHAT YOU GOT
> THEN BLAH . . . BLAH . . . BLAH . . .

*(The radio goes to static. Dina goes to her window and looks
out at the Telephone Guy, who waits by the lonely pay phone.)*

(Calling out the window) Nu, hee tsiltselah? [Well, did she
call yet?]

(The Telephone Guy looks up.)

TELEPHONE GUY: *Od lo, Dina! Aval* [Not yet, Dina! But] soon!
Soon!

(Dina turns to her guests.)

DINA: You see this boy? Every night he waits his girlfriend to
call. A month now like this. He wait and wait and wait.
(Pause) Maybe, if you want later, we can go out a little.

TEWFIQ: No, thank you, madam. It's too late.

DINA: No big deal. Just show around. There is a place, not far
from here. Nice, some food, some drink.

TEWFIQ: I don't know.

HALED *(To Tewfiq): Az-sit owza turuah.Yallah khud-ha.* [The lady
wants to go out. Take her out.]

DINA: You want to come too, Haled?

HALED (*Smiling at Tewfiq*): No thank you, madam. I'll stay.

DINA: So it's decide, General. You and me.

(*Transition . . .*)

Scene 5

Lights up in Itzik and Iris's apartment. Itzik and Iris sit in awkward silence at the dinner table with Camal and Simon. Iris's father, Avrum, is also here. Iris is silently fuming. A few beats like this. Then:

AVRUM: *Where* you are from?
CAMAL/SIMON: Egypt.
AVRUM: Egypt! Wow!

    (A few more beats.)

ITZIK *(Pointing at his wife)*: My wife has birthday today.
SIMON: Oh! Happy birthday!
IRIS: Thank you.
SIMON: Many happy years.
IRIS: Thank you.
ITZIK *(To Iris)*: *At ro'a? Hem lo kol kach gru'eem.* [See? They're not so bad.]
IRIS: *Ken* [Yes], let's invite them every night.

(Baby cries.)

ITZIK: *At rotsa sheh—?* [Do you want—?]
IRIS: *Ta'azov.* [Leave it.]

(Iris goes to the other room to deal with it.)

AVRUM *(To the Band)*: So! What do you do in the orchestra?
SIMON: I play the clarinet. And also I conduct.

(Camal snorts derisively.)

Well, sometimes.
ITZIK *(Indicating Simon)*: You know, he wrote concerto.
AVRUM: Concerto?
SIMON: No, no—
ITZIK: Before, in the restaurant, he played for me.
SIMON: It's not real concerto.
AVRUM: Concerto! Wow! Wow! Wow!
SIMON: I didn't finish. *(To Itzik)* And you . . . work in the restaurant, or—?
ITZIK: Em, no, I am . . . between works now.
IRIS *(Scoffing)*: Between.
ITZIK: Between for a while.
SIMON *(To Iris)*: And . . . you? What you do?
IRIS: I care for invalids. All day and all night.
SIMON: Oh. Okay.

(A moment. Then:)

AVRUM: You know: I also play with band. I play . . . *kinor.*
ITZIK: Violin.
AVRUM: Violin. I play in wedding, bar mitzvahs. All songs, Beatles, Rolling Stone. Klezmer. It's how I meet my wife. Iris mother.
IRIS *(Quietly)*: *Aba.* [Dad.]
AVRUM: *Hakol beseder, zeh beseder.* [Everything's okay, it's okay.]
IRIS: *Iti zeh lo beseder.* [It's not okay with me.]

(Beat.)

CAMAL: Where your wife is now?

(Simon looks at Camal like, "Are you kidding me?")

AVRUM: She pass away.

(Simon buries his face in his hands. Then:)

SIMON: Very sorry.
CAMAL: When?
AVRUM: Last year.
SIMON *(To Camal)*: *Enta mushkiltak eeeh, ya ehbal?* [What is wrong with you, you idiot?]
AVRUM: It's okay.
SIMON *(Back to Avrum)*: No. You don't have to talk about.
AVRUM: I don't mind to talk about. *(Beat)* We meet in the nightclub. The calypso. I was playing and peoples is dancing and suddenly . . . I see her. And I stop. *(Beat)* For three, four minutes. I was like stone. And the band is play, you know what is em: "Summertime . . . nananana . . ."

(Camal joins in.)

AVRUM/CAMAL: ". . . is easy."

(Itzik joins in, too.)

AVRUM/CAMAL/ITZIK: "Fish are jumpin' . . . and the cotton is high . . ."

(Simon finally joins in. The singing becomes quite spirited, un-self-conscious.)

ALL MEN: "Oh your dad is rich . . . and your mom is good-looking . . ."

(Avrum drops out on this lyric, going into a reverie.)

SIMON/ITZIK/CAMAL: "... so hush little baby ... don't you cry ..."

AVRUM:

> SHE WAS IN A WHITE DRESS
> WITH RED AND PURPLE RIBBONS IN HER HAIR.
> SHE WAS DANCING WITH SOMEBODY
> BUT IN LOVE AND MUSIC, ALL IS FAIR.
>
> WE WERE FINISHING "THE GIRL FROM IPANEMA,"
> GOING INTO "SUMMERTIME."
> I WAS IN THE MIDDLE OF MY SOLO
> WHEN HER EYES MET MINE.
>
> LOVE STARTS ON A DOWNBEAT.
> LOVE STARTS WHEN THE MUSIC STARTS.
> LOVE STARTS WHEN THE TUNE IS SWEET
> AND YOU LIFT YOUR FEET
> TO THE BEAT OF YOUR HEART.
>
> LOVE MAKES A RHYTHM.
> LOVE DANCES IN A DANCER'S SHOES.
> IT MOVES WHEN YOU START TO MOVE
> AND WHAT IS THE GROOVE?
> THE BEAT OF YOUR HEART.
>
> AND WE PLAYED "MOON RIVER"
> AND "I WANT TO HOLD YOUR HAND"
> AND THE GIRL IN THE WHITE DRESS
> AND THE RIBBONS IN HER HAIR
> DANCED TO MY BAND.
>
> AND I COULD FEEL MY HEART,
> IT STARTED JUMPING IN MY CHEST
> AND I SMILED AT HER AND SHE SMILED AT ME
> AND THE MUSIC DID THE REST.

(Avrum gets up from the table.)

LOVE SPARKS ON THE UPBEAT,
IGNITING WITH A MINOR NINTH,
RESOLVING TO A MAJOR SIX
THEN SOMETHING CLICKS
AND EVERYTHING STARTS.

THERE GOES THE KICK DRUM
SPELLING OUT THE RHYTHM OF LOVE,
TELLING YOU TO GET OFF YOUR SEAT
AND MOVE YOUR FEET.
AND DANCE TO THE BEAT OF YOUR HEART.

(Simon joins in drumming with Avrum. So does Itzik. They dance, during which Camal takes out his violin and plays.)

AND IF YOU PLAY ME "SUMMERTIME"
AND IF I STOP AND CLOSE MY EYES
I'LL SEE AN ANGEL SWIRLING,
MOVING, YOUNG AND SO ALIVE.

THIS MUSIC IS A TIME MACHINE
THIS MUSIC IS A GIFT FROM GOD.
HER FACE WAS BEAUTIFUL
MY GOD, HER FACE WAS BEAUTIFUL.

SO MAYBE I'M ROMANTIC.
MAYBE I'M A SENTIMENTAL FOOL.
MAYBE MUSIC IS THE FOOD OF LOVE
BUT MUSIC AND LOVE, WHO CAN TELL THEM APART?

AVRUM:
JUST LET ME HEAR THE DOWNBEAT

SIMON/CAMAL/ITZIK:
LET ME HEAR THE
DOWNBEAT.

AND LET ME HEAR THE BUM, BUM,
BUM

BUM, BUM, BUM

33

AVRUM (*Continued*):
> AND LET ME HEAR YOU KICK THE KICK
> AND WHACK THE SNARE
> AND SHAKE YOUR ASS AND STIR UP THE AIR
> AND DANCE WITH THE GIRL WITH THE RIBBONS IN
>   HER HAIR—

ALL MEN:
> EMBRACING THE RHYTHM OF LOVE
> THAT'S EXACTLY THE SAME
> AS THE BEAT OF YOUR

AVRUM:
> HEART!

CAMAL:
> THE BEAT OF YOUR HEART

SIMON/ITZIK:
> THE BEAT OF YOUR HEART

SIMON/CAMAL/ITZIK:
> THE BEAT OF YOUR HEART!

> (*Transition, during which we see Dina, in a dress, getting ready to go out . . .*)

SCENE 6

Dina's place. Dina is finishing getting ready, in her bathroom mirror. During this, Tewfiq comes to stand in the doorway and freezes, like stone, staring at her. Dina turns and sees Tewfiq.

DINA: How do I look?

TEWFIQ: Very fine indeed.

DINA: Would you say if you thought otherwise? (*Beat*) Don't you want to take your hat off?

TEWFIQ: What?

DINA: It's very hot with hat. You can take it off.

(A moment. Tewfiq takes his hat off.)

It's better, no? A man should not hide behind his hat.

(Dina leads Tewfiq out of her apartment. The other Band Members—the ones who remained at the café—are sitting around outside, smoking, playing backgammon. As Dina

and Tewfiq walk away from her place, they pass the Tele-
phone Guy, waiting by the phone.)

Did she call yet?
TELEPHONE GUY: Not yet. But soon! Soon!

(Dina and Tewfiq exit. Then Camal enters, looking over his
shoulder to make sure no one has seen him come to the phone.
Then he waits, assuming the Telephone Guy is going to use it.
Then he realizes the Telephone Guy is just standing there.)

CAMAL: I was hope to use the phone. *(Pause)* My embassy will
    close. *(Pause)* So . . . I can use it? Or—
TELEPHONE GUY: It is broken.
CAMAL: What?
TELEPHONE GUY: Not working.

(Camal is confused. Then he picks up the phone to "test" it.
It's working. Camal dials and steps to the side to have privacy
for the call. Through the following, the Telephone Guy waits
impatiently—perhaps even disruptively.)

CAMAL: *Aloo, hel maee es-sefara el-mesriya? Ma'ak Camal Abdel-*
    Azim, min el-firqa el-musiqiyah el-mesriya min ashurta el-
    a'askariya bil-iskandariya. Ehna mahsureen. Beit Hatik-
    fah. (Beat) Beit Hatikfah. (Beat) Beh, Beh, Beh . . . Aywa,
    kalimni tany a'al-nimra di: (He reads off the phone) Sifr-
    saba'a-khamsa-waehid-sitta-sifr-tisa'a-sifr-sifr. Shukran, ma'a-
    salama. [Hello, is this the Egyptian embassy? This is
    Camal Abdel-Azim, with the Alexandria Ceremonial Police
    Orchestra. We are stranded. Bet Hatikvah. Bet Hatik-
    vah. Beh, Beh, Beh . . . Yes, call me back at this number:
    075160900. Thank you. Goodbye.]

(Camal hangs up. The Telephone Guy instantly picks up the
receiver to make sure it's still working, hangs up again, and
resumes waiting.)

They will . . . call back. So.

36

(Camal leaves. Papi emerges from the closed café. Haled, who has perhaps been lurking in the shadows for some time, sees him.)

PAPI *(To Musicians hanging out)*: So, good night.
HALED: Going out?
PAPI *(To himself)*: *Oy, lo.* [Oh no.]

(Beat.)

HALED: Going out? Good time?

(Beat.)

PAPI: You can go in.
HALED: What?
PAPI: You can go in. Your friends are there.
HALED: Oh, no. Maybe I . . . With you. I don't sleep, so maybe I go with you, like tourist. Have a look on the city.
PAPI: Ah, no, em—

(Zelger enters.)

ZELGER: Who wants to party!
PAPI: *Lo.* [No.]
ZELGER: *Maztomeret, "lo"? Yehiyeh gadol!* [What do you mean "no"? It's gonna be great!]
PAPI: *Hoo yirtze la'vo itanu!* [He's going to want to come with us!] *(To Haled)* Okay, good night.
HALED *(To Zelger, offering his hand for a handshake)*: Haled.
ZELGER *(Shaking his hand)*: Zelger.
PAPI: Um—
ZELGER: I like your clothes.
HALED: Yes. Like Michael Jackson. So I come?
PAPI: Only two girls! *(Beat)* Okay?
HALED *(Understanding)*: Ah.

(Zelger shrugs, apologetically.)

PAPI: Yes, so . . .

HALED: Okay. No problem. I just look on the city.

(*Before Papi can protest again, Zelger points out that the two girls, Anna and Julia, are approaching. During the following, Julia pulls Anna aside for a very similar conversation to the one Papi and Zelger are having. Only Haled sees this.*)

ZELGER: *Heene hen ba'ot.* [Here they come.]

PAPI: *Zot habat doda?* [That's the cousin?]

ZELGER: *Ken. Mah.* [Yes. What.]

PAPI: *Hee ha'atsuva hazot!* [She's that gloomy girl!]

ZELGER: *Hee lo atzuva!* [She's not gloomy!]

PAPI: *Ken nachon!* [Yes!]

HALED: Something is wrong?

PAPI: Ehh, I know this girl. She is so gloomy, no smile!

HALED: You want I talk to her?

PAPI: No!

ZELGER: *Sheket, hen ba'ot!* [Quiet, here they come!]

(*Indeed, Anna has now successfully dragged Julia toward the boys.*)

ANNA: *Hi Motek.* [Hi Sweetie.]

ZELGER: *Eze cooseet.* [What a nice piece of ass.]

(*They kiss.*)

ANNA: *Shalom, Papi. Zot Julia.* [Hello, Papi. This is Julia.]

(*Anna shoves Julia slightly forward.*)

JULIA: *Shalom, Papi.* [Hello.]

(*An awkward moment as Papi says nothing. Then the nearby Band Members begin to play.*)

ZELGER: *Yallah alachnu.* [Let's go.]

(Zelger, Anna, Haled, Julia and Papi begin to exit. As they go:)

ANNA *(Indicating Haled)*: *Aval mi zeh ha ish hazeh?* [But who's this guy?]

ZELGER *(Shrugging)*: *Haver shel Papi.* [A friend of Papi's.]

(When they're gone, the Band Members outside the café continue to play . . .
Musical interlude: "Soraya.")

Scene 7

. . . And as the interlude ends, the music becomes the music on a jukebox. Ugly fluorescent lights up on a cafeteria seating area. Dina and Tewfiq enter, holding trays of food, like high school students looking for a place to sit. Dina leads Tewfiq over to a table and they sit. Tewfiq looks around, awkwardly, at some staring people.

DINA: Everything's okay?

TEWFIQ: Yes, it's just . . . People are staring.

DINA: Leave it. People here are in the Stone Age. You know? Just . . .
    (Beat) Tell me something in Arabic.

TEWFIQ: Ehhh . . . *(Struggles for words)*

DINA: I don't know, just something. To hear the music.

(A moment.)

TEWFIQ: *Fi shita', khuz shamsiya. Fi saif, irtadee qoobaa ala ra'sak. Fil khareef, ibqa fee baytak.*

(Beat.)

DINA: What does it mean?

TEWFIQ: In wintertime, take an umbrella. In summertime, put a hat on your head. In autumntime, stay at home.

(A moment.)

DINA: So . . . what do you play in the orchestra? You play, like, army music? *(She makes the sounds of rapid snare drumming)*

TEWFIQ: No, no. We are traditional orchestra. We play classical Arab music.

DINA: What, like, Oum Kalthoum? Farid?

TEWFIQ: You think it's silly.

DINA: No.

TEWFIQ: No? You like Oum Kalthoum?

DINA: Yes!

TEWFIQ: No.

DINA: Yes! Don't tell me what I like! She is one of my favorite singer. *(Beat)* When I was a girl we used to have here Arab music, Egyptian music, on the radio. And on TV, Egyptian movies, every Friday afternoon. This . . . mysterious people I would never meet, but who came to me, through the speakers, through the screen.

> OUM KALTHOUM AND OMAR SHARIF
> CAME FLOATING ON A JASMINE WIND.
> FROM THE WEST, FROM THE SOUTH—
> HONEY IN MY EARS,
> SPICE IN MY MOUTH.
>
> DARK AND THRILLING, STRANGE AND SWEET.
> CLEOPATRA AND A HANDSOME THIEF
> AND THEY FLOATED IN
> ON A JASMINE WIND
> OUM KALTHOUM AND OMAR SHARIF
> AND THEY FLOATED IN

ON A JASMINE WIND
OUM KALTHOUM AND OMAR SHARIF.

The best movie was, *River of Love*? Where they meet on the
train, she is reading, and he says—
TEWFIQ: "A book is a loyal companion always."
DINA: You know it!
TEWFIQ: Oh. Yes.

DINA:

FRIDAY EVENING, OMAR SHARIF,
IN BLACK AND WHITE AND BLURRY THROUGH TEARS.
MY MOTHER AND I WOULD SIT THERE IN A TRANCE.
HE WAS COOL TO THE MARROW
THE PHARAOH OF ROMANCE.

SUNDAY MORNING, OUM KALTHOUM.
HER VOICE WOULD FILL OUR LIVING ROOM.
THE SHIP FROM EGYPT ALWAYS CAME
SAILING IN ON RADIO WAVES

AND THE JASMINE WIND,
DEEP PERFUME.
OO OO OO OO OUM KALTHOUM—

*(During the following, the ugly cafeteria is subtly transformed:
everyone becomes somehow beautiful. Everyone is in love.)*

AND THE LIVING ROOM BECOMES A GARDEN
AND THE TV SET BECOMES THE FOUNTAIN
AND THE MUSIC FLOWS
IN THE GARDEN
AND EVERYTHING GROWS.

OUM KALTHOUM AND OMAR SHARIF
CAME FLOATING ON A LEMON LEAF,
FLYING IN ON A JASMINE WIND,
OUM KALTHOUM AND OMAR SHARIF

AND WE DANCED WITH THEM IN A JASMINE-SCENTED
  WIND,
OUM KALTHOUM AND OMAR SHARIF.

TEWFIQ: Not everybody feels like you.
DINA: What do you mean?
TEWFIQ: Music. Stories. Today it is not that important. People
  care about other things. Money, efficiency, worth.
DINA: People are stupid, aren't they?
TEWFIQ: Yes. They are sometimes.

(*A moment between them. Then Dina sees something: Sammy
and his wife entering, at a distance, with a stroller.*)

DINA: *Ben zona.* [Sonofabitch.]
TEWFIQ: What?
DINA: I said, "Sonofabitch."
TEWFIQ: Oh. (*Beat*) I don't know this movie . . .
DINA (*Pointing*): You see this guy? There, with his family? Nice
  wife, nice children, everything nice nice?
TEWFIQ: Yes.
DINA: He is someone who . . . He and I sometimes . . . (*Beat*)
  You know?

(*Beat.*)

TEWFIQ (*Uncomfortably*): Oh.
DINA: And this? Is a place he knows sometimes I go.
TEWFIQ: Oh. (*Beat*) Well—
DINA: Let's meet him. (*Calling and waving*) Sammy! Is that you?
TEWFIQ: What you are doing?
DINA: It's fine. Sammy!
SAMMY'S WIFE: *Zot Dina?* [Is that Dina?]
SAMMY: *Ken. Ma?* [Yes. What?]
SAMMY'S WIFE: *Ma hi rotza?* [What does she want?]
SAMMY: *Ani yodeah? Betach mashehoo im ha inventory.* [How do
  I know? Probably something with the inventory.]
DINA: *Bo, bo! Tagid shalom!* [Come, come! Say hello!] Here he
  comes.

(Sammy is indeed approaching.)

SAMMY: *Ma at osa? Hishta'gat?!* [What are you doing? Are you crazy?!]
DINA: Hello, Sammy. Out for a nice dinner with your family?
SAMMY: *Ma?* [What?]
DINA: I am out for a nice dinner also. With my good friend Tewfiq.

(Dina gestures to Tewfiq. A moment.)

TEWFIQ: Hello.
DINA: He is visiting, by special invitation, from Egypt, for a big concert. I am speaking English, not to be rude, so he can understand.
SAMMY *(To Tewfiq)*: Okay. Very nice meet you. *(To Dina) Hee ratsta lavo henah. Ma yacholti la'asot?* [She wanted to come here. What could I do?]
DINA: Yes, fine, no problem. Why are you getting so upset?
SAMMY: *Beseder, maspeek.* [Fine, enough.] *(To Tewfiq)* I go back now.

(Sammy exits. A moment.)

DINA: Sonofabitch.

(It occurs to Tewfiq it might be a good idea to leave.)

TEWFIQ: Em, perhaps we should—
DINA: Excuse me.

(Dina gets up and goes to a jukebox and puts on a song—an Oum Kalthoum song—and walks back over to Tewfiq. Then she sits, facing away from him, and mimes holding a book. What's she doing? Then:)

Say it again.
TEWFIQ: What?

DINA: Say it again.

(A moment. Then he understands.)

TEWFIQ: "A book is a loyal companion always."
DINA: "This one is unrealistic. A woman give up her child. A man dies for love."
TEWFIQ: "Ah but: love in itself *is* hope. And hope is a reality in our lives. Who can live without hope?"

(Dina smiles at him. The Band Members outside the café begin to play again . . .
    Musical interlude: "Haj-Butrus.")

Scene 8

. . . And as the interlude reaches its end, lights up on Itzik and Iris's place, where Simon is playing for them. He finishes as the interlude does. Itzik, Iris and Avrum all applaud. This dies down. Then:

AVRUM *(To Simon)*: Hey! Your concerto. Play it for us.
ITZIK/SIMON: Oh yes!/No.
ITZIK/AVRUM: Yes, it's so nice!/Why no?
SIMON: It's only prelude for overture and I didn't finish.
ITZIK *(To the others)*: It's so nice.
AVRUM: So? Play it.
ITZIK/AVRUM *(A chant)*: Play it, play it, play it. Yayyyyyy!

> *(This "Yay" as Simon picks up his clarinet. Then he plays the concerto as Avrum, Itzik and Iris listen. It cuts off as before. A moment.)*

AVRUM: That's it?
SIMON: I didn't finish.

AVRUM: Why not?
SIMON: I . . . don't know.

(*Beat.*)

AVRUM: You must finish!
SIMON: I know.

(*Beat.*)

AVRUM: Why you don't finish?
SIMON: I don't know! I . . . I begin it at the academy? But then
    my wife get pregnant and life and time . . .
IRIS (*A grunt*): Hnn.
ITZIK: You know, once, when I was child, I miss my own birth-
    day. My mother is make . . . a party? And while I wait,
    I climb a tree. And it is so . . . nice up there. The wind. The
    sky. I don't want to come down. The whole village is look
    for me. I don't come. I hear people call my name. I don't
    answer. I stay all day. I miss my birthday. Maybe, for you,
    not finish is like this. You are in the tree. You don't want to
    come down.
IRIS: No. He don't stay up there because it's so nice. He *hide*
    in his tree. Because he is afraid of his birthday. Afraid to
    grow up.

(*A beat. Then:*)

Ani yotzet. [I'm going out.]

(*Iris goes to grab her coat and heads for the door. Itzik fol-
lows her.*)

ITZIK: But . . . we have guests.
IRIS (*Turning back*): Ah, ken, nachon. [Oh, yes, right.] (*To Simon*)
    Very sorry, but I go now.
AVRUM: *Iris, boi, shvi, ze beseder.* [Iris, come, sit, it's okay.]
IRIS: *Lo, Aba.* [No, Dad.]

SIMON: Would you like us to go?

IRIS: No it's not you. It's this boy. Who is still up in his tree. All his life, up in his tree, and never coming down!

(Now Itzik switches to Hebrew for privacy . . .)

ITZIK: *Iris, tagidi li, ma cara*— [Iris, tell me, what happened—]

(. . . But by now Iris has gotten going in English. Thus:)

IRIS: No! I don't know now what I saw in you! I don't know if I have anything left for you in my heart!

(Iris walks out. Itzik stands there, stunned. We follow Iris as she paces outside, lights a cigarette, sits . . . We hear a techno beat and then . . .)

Scene 9

Zelger whizzes by on roller skates. We are in the roller rink. Corny roller rink music. A DJ. Reflection from a mirror ball. Anna joins Zelger, skating. As they make a couple of circuits of the rink:

ZELGER: *Heene hee!* [There she is!]
ANNA: *Barur!* [Clearly!]
ZELGER: *Mami, eeshtapart!* [Sweetie, you've gotten better!]
ANNA: *Malka!* [Queen!]

> *(Julia skates by as well here. Then Papi. Each alone and awkward. Then Haled enters. A Security Guard calls to Haled.)*

GUARD: *Allo, allo! Mi ata?* [Hello, hello! Who are you?] *(Beat)* Who you? What you doing here?
HALED: I am . . . visit. I am musician.
GUARD: You are musician.
HALED: Yes.
GUARD: Play something.
HALED: What?

GUARD: *Play* something.

HALED: Okay but . . . I am professional.

GUARD: Okay . . . ?

HALED: So you will have to pay me.

(*A moment. The Guard steps forward, threateningly . . . but then Papi steps in.*)

PAPI (*Gently*): Allo! Allo! Ze beseder, hoo chaver sheli, okay? [Hey, it's okay, he is a friend of mine, okay?]

GUARD: Im mashe'hoo koreh ze alecha. [If something happens, it's on you.]

PAPI: Okay.

(*A moment. The Guard walks away.*)

HALED: Thank you.

PAPI (*Shrugging*): That guy . . . Asshole.

HALED: And . . . thank you for invite me here.

PAPI: Oh. Welcome.

(*Zelger skates up to them.*)

ZELGER (*To Haled*): You like? I am investor! Maybe later we talk about you invest too, yes? Yes!

(*Zelger skates off. Then Julia skates past again, staring shyly at Papi. Papi freezes and looks away. Julia skates off. Haled sees all this.*)

HALED: You don't go with girls too much, eh?

PAPI: No. You go with girls all the time, yes?

HALED: It's not so simple.

PAPI: Why no?

HALED: You know what is . . . arrange marriage?

PAPI: You are married?

HALED: No but . . . my parents, they chose the girl, and when I go back from this trip . . . (*Beat*) So you and girl never . . . You never?

PAPI: No. I hear the sea.
HALED: What?
PAPI: I hear sea. In my ears. (*Then, demonstrating*) Chuuuuuuu . . .

> I DON'T KNOW WITH THE GIRLS.
> I DON'T KNOW WHAT TO DO,
> I DON'T KNOW WHERE TO START.
> I'M SMARTER UP HERE THAN I AM DOWN HERE
> AND UP HERE I'M NOT TOO SMART.
>
> THEY MIGHT SAY ONE THING OR ANOTHER.
> THEY MIGHT HAVE SMILED AT ME ONCE OR TWICE.
> IF THEY HAVE BREASTS AND THEY'RE NOT MY MOTHER
> THEN ALL I HEAR IS CHUUUUUUUUUU . . .

(*Julia skates by again, staring. Then:*)

> AND THE HANDS GET HEAVY, OH THE HANDS,
> I DON'T KNOW WHAT TO DO WITH THE HANDS OR THE
>   FEET.
> FROZEN IN FEAR LIKE A DEER WITH THE LIGHTS
> IN THE EYES IN THE MIDDLE OF THE STREET.
>
> SHE MIGHT BE WANTING TO GET TOUCHY-FEELY,
> SHE MIGHT BE TALKING TO ME REALLY NICE,
> SHE MIGHT AS WELL BE SPEAKING SWAHILI
> 'CAUSE ALL I HEAR IS CHUUUUUUU
>
> AND MY TONGUE GETS BIG
> AND I CAN'T MOVE MY KNEES
> AND MY EYEBALLS FREEZE
> AND ALL I SEE'S A TUNNEL
> AND THERE'S COTTON IN MY HEAD,
> MY LEGS ARE FULL OF LEAD
> AND MY BRAIN GOES DEADER
> THAN THE DEAD SEA.
> DEAD DEAD DEAD
> IN THE MIND AND I FIND

THAT I KIND OF GO
INTO AN INFANTILE TRANCE.
I'M PEEING IN MY—NOT LITERALLY PEEING IN MY—
BUT, YOU KNOW, I MAY AS WELL BE PEEING IN MY—
THEN I LOSE MY WITS, MY LIGHTS GO OFF,
I'LL GET ALL STICKY IN THE PITS,
I SMELL LIKE FALAFEL
AND MY EARS GET HOT
AND I FEEL REAL AWFUL
AND ALL I HEAR IS . . .

(Julia stops nearby.)

JULIA: *Bo Papi. Ta'seh iti skehtim.* [Come on, Papi. Skate with me.]
PAPI: *Lo toda.* [No thanks.]
JULIA *(Taking his hand)*: *Nu, bo.* [Come on.]
PAPI: *Lo, be'emet, ze beseder.* [No, really, it's okay.]
JULIA: *Bo!* [*Come!*]

(Papi jerks his arm back. Julia falls to the floor. A terrible, frozen moment. Then Julia starts to wail and everyone rushes forward, variously, to curse Papi and help Julia. All at once:)

ANNA: *Ma aseeta la, ata mifager? At beseder Julia? Ma aseeta la, ata dafooq ba rosh? Allo, Papi, ani medaberet eetcha, dachafta ota, o ma? Ata mamash dafooq ba rosh, coos emech.* [What did you do to her, are you retarded? Are you okay, Julia? What did you do to her, are you fucked in the head? Hello, Papi, I'm talking to you, did you push her or what? You really are fucked in the head, you motherfucker.]
ZELGER *(During this, skating over with a small first aid kit)*: It's okay. It's okay. It's okay.
GUARD *(During this, helping Julia up)*: *Ma kara? Ma kara, ya manyak? Idyot! Boi motek. Boi. Lo kara shoomdavar. Yallah! Achat, shtayim ve sha—opalah!* [What happened? What happened, you maniac? Idiot! Come on sweetheart. Come on. Nothing happened. Let's go! One, two and thr—opalah!]

(A moment as the others tend to Julia, and Papi stands frozen. Then:)

PAPI:

DEAD DEAD DEAD,
BELLY UP, GOING 'ROUND,
SINKING DOWN DOWN DOWN
LIKE A SCHMUCK.
DEAD IN THE HEAD,
DEAD IN THE WATER,
DEAD IN A MAGICAL SEA FULL OF SUCK.

GO AHEAD AND TELL ME I SHOULD KEEP ON TRYING,
GO AHEAD AND TELL ME I SHOULD BREAK THE ICE.
I'LL BE STANDING HERE DEAF AND DYING
AND ALL I'LL HEAR IS CHUUUUUUUUU . . .

(Papi stares into space, despairing. Then the DJ changes the music and . . .)

HALED:

NOT BREAK THE ICE,
YOU MELT THE ICE.
YOU MELT YOURSELF
AND SOON YOU'RE ALL ONE PUDDLE.

YOU TALK, SHE TALKS—
IT'S NOT ABOUT THE CONVERSATION.
THE WORDS ARE LIKE YOUR LIPS
ARE REACHING OUT
TO KISS THE EAR.

YOU'RE HERE, SHE'S HERE,
TWO DROPS OF WATER.
THE PULL, THE PULL,
INVISIBLE BUT REALLY REAL.

> YOUR EYES, HER EYES
> AND SOON YOU'RE LOOKING IN A MIRROR.
> YOU REALIZE YOU CAN'T GET NEARER,
> YOU ARE BOTH RIGHT THERE.

(Haled encourages Papi to go toward Julia. He takes a step, then turns back.)

PAPI: I can't. I hear the sea.
HALED: Then walk into the sea.

(Papi goes to sit next to Julia. He does nothing. Haled sighs and sits next to Papi, and puts his arm around him. Understanding, Papi puts his arm around Julia. Papi looks to Haled again. Haled puts a hand on Papi's knee and massages it. Papi puts a hand on Julia's knee and massages it. Julia looks at Papi. Papi removes Haled's hand from his own knee.)

> YOU GLOW, SHE GLOWS—
> TWO SUNS, NO SHADOW.
> YOUR SKIN, HER SKIN
> AND EVERYTHING'S ALL LIGHT.
>
> NO EDGE, NO EDGE,
> NO WALLS, NO BORDER,
> TWO STREAMS OF WATER
> THAT BECOME THE SEA . . .

(By now, Papi and Julia are skating around together as Haled watches.)

HALED:
> THE DANCE, THE DANCE,
> YOU SEE, THE WIND THAT MOVES
>   THE TREES IS

PAPI:
> THE DANCE,
>   THE DANCE

> THE ALGEBRA THAT MOVES YOUR KNEES
> IS WRITTEN IN HER EYES.

HER EYES, YOUR EYES
YOU'RE ONLY LOOKING IN
   A MIRROR.

HER EYES, YOUR EYES
YOU'RE ONLY LOOK-
   ING IN A MIRROR.

YOU REALIZE YOU CAN'T GET NEARER
AND THERE'S NOWHERE YOU DON'T MEET . . .

*(Papi and Julia embrace and . . . Transition . . . The roller
rink fades away, some of the Band Members appear and we
are in . . .)*

SCENE 10

An empty concrete park. A lonely bench. Dina and Tewfiq enter.
Some of the Band Members are visible in the shadows—there,
but not really there. They gently underscore the following:

DINA: This is the park. It's not look like a park. You have to imag-
ine. *(She points)* You see? This is the grass. And there? It's
where the children play. And this? This is the sea. Do you
hear the sea?

TEWFIQ: Yes.

DINA: Tell me, Tewfiq, how does it feel. I mean, to do music, to
have the orchestra. How does it feel?

(Tewfiq struggles.)

To have all the people waiting for you, and all the eyes for
you, and . . . You know . . . ?

TEWFIQ: It's, em . . .

DINA: Yes? What.

(Tewfiq gives up on speaking. As he lifts his hands in a conducting gesture, the music swells. He holds them up. It swells further. Then he drops his hands. Silence. Dina repeats the gesture.)

It feels like the most important thing in the world.

TEWFIQ: No, the most important thing in the world is fishing.

DINA: What? Fishing? No, it's so boring!

TEWFIQ: It's not!

DINA: Yes it is. So boring.

TEWFIQ: It's not boring at all. It's the sound of water, and waves . . . distant children playing on the beach . . . and the sound of the bait, falling in the water. In the early hours, on the sea, you can hear the whole world like . . . like symphony. *(A beat. Then)* Before, when . . . my wife was alive, I used to take home, and she used to cook. But now I just put them back.

DINA: Your wife is dead?

TEWFIQ: Yes.

DINA: Was it . . . long time ago, or . . . ?

TEWFIQ: Almost three years. September twenty-one. September.

DINA: I'm sorry from asking something that . . . hurts.

TEWFIQ: No, it's okay. They say it's good, sometimes, to talk about things.

DINA: Yes. *(Beat)* She was pretty?

TEWFIQ: Yes.

DINA: Did she like fishing?

TEWFIQ *(He laughs)*: No. Not at all.

(They laugh together.)

DINA: How did you meet?

TEWFIQ: We met in the academy. At a friend's house. She came with her friends. You know, we talked. She laughed at me, with her friends. I thought she didn't like me. But, after few days, she came to see me play a concert.

DINA: She see you conduct.

TEWFIQ: Yes and, I think, that night I sing.

DINA: What? You sing?

TEWFIQ: On . . . some song, yes.

DINA: Sing for me.

TEWFIQ: What? No.

DINA: Please?

TEWFIQ: It is in Arabic.

DINA: So?

TEWFIQ: I have not done it. For long time.

DINA: Then it will be very special for me.

(Tewfiq still seems resistant. Then Dina makes the conducting gesture he taught her. Tewfiq begins to sing.)

TEWFIQ:

    ITGARA'A

    ITGARA'A

    ITGARA'A

    ITGARA'A

    MIN EL WIHDA

    MIN EL FARAH

    ITGARA'A

    ITGARAHOUM

    INTA EL WIHDA

    INTA EL FARAH

    ITGARAHOUM

DINA:

    IS THIS A HYMN? IS THIS A LOVE SONG?

    SOMETHING ANCIENT BY A POET, MAYBE HAFIZ? MAYBE
        RUMI?

    IS HE SINGING ABOUT TWO HEARTS SEARCHING IN
        THE DARKNESS?

    OR IS HE SINGING ABOUT FISHING?

    THE TUNE SEEMS SAD BUT ARE THE WORDS SAD?

    WHAT'S HE SAYING? IS HE PRAYING? AND WHY DOES IT
        GET TO ME?

IS HE LONELY, MAYBE REACHING OUT FOR SOMEONE?
LOOK AT ME, MAYBE I'M THE ONE WHO'S FISHING.

EVERY DAY YOU STARE TO THE WEST, TO THE SOUTH
YOU CAN SEE FOR MILES BUT THINGS NEVER CHANGE
THEN HONEY IN YOUR EARS, SPICE IN YOUR MOUTH—

NOTHING'S AS SURPRISING AS THE TASTE OF
SOMETHING STRANGE

AND HERE'S THIS MAN RIGHT HERE BESIDE ME,
KIND OF DEEP AND KIND OF CUTE IN HIS SERGEANT
PEPPER SUIT.
IS THIS MY SHEIK? IS THIS MY OMAR SHARIF?
WELL I KNOW IT'S SOMETHING DIFFERENT.

TEWFIQ:

ITGARA'A

TEWFIQ/DINA:

LA DA DA DA DA DA DA DA DAAAAA DA
LA DA DA DA DA DA DA DA DAAAAA DA . . .

DINA:

WHO IS THIS MAN RIGHT HERE BESIDE ME?
CLOSER BY AN INCH OR TWO MY CHEEK WOULD
TOUCH HIS EAR.
WHAT IS HE THINKING? WHAT DOES HE WISH FOR?
IS HE SINGING ABOUT WISHING?

SOMETHING NEW I'VE NEVER SEEN BEFORE
THROUGH THESE WALLS I BUILD, THESE GATES
I PROTECT.
SOMETHING NEW I DIDN'T NOTICE I'VE BEEN HOPING
FOR.

NOTHING IS AS BEAUTIFUL AS SOMETHING THAT YOU
DON'T EXPECT.

LOOK AT THOSE HANDS—THOSE ARE NOT YOUNG
   HANDS
BUT THEY MOVE LIKE THEY ARE SWIMMING THROUGH
   THE MUSIC,
THROUGH THE MUSIC,
AND I DON'T KNOW WHAT I FEEL
AND I DON'T KNOW WHAT I KNOW.
ALL I KNOW IS I FEEL SOMETHING DIFFERENT.

TEWFIQ:

ITGARAHOUM

DINA:

HE MAKES ME FEEL SOMETHING DIFFERENT.

(A moment.)

Did you have children?

TEWFIQ: Yes we had . . . one son.

DINA: Just one? Big man, Arabic, family, and only one son? *(Off Tewfiq's awkwardness)* I'm joking.

TEWFIQ: It's okay.

(A moment. Dina is about to ask something else when . . . Sammy enters.)

SAMMY: *Eene at.* [There you are.]

DINA: Oh god.

SAMMY: *Ma le'azazel aseet sham? Ma, nafalt al harosh?* [The hell were you doing back there? What, did you fall on your head?]

TEWFIQ: Hey—

SAMMY: Stay out of it, it's not your business.

DINA: *I was eating dinner.*

SAMMY: *Achshav eeshti sho'elet milion she'elot beglal hashtooyot shelach!* [Now my wife is asking millions of questions because of your nonsense!]

DINA: He says his wife is ask lots of questions now thanks to me.

SAMMY: *Lama at . . . ? Tafseeki letargem lo!* [Why do you . . . ? Stop translating for him!] *(To Tewfiq)* It's not your business.
TEWFIQ: I know.
DINA: You make it his business because you follow us!
TEWFIQ: Hey—
DINA: *Ma evetah otah l'sham? Chashavta eich ani yirgish? Ze mavich! Ze hamakom sheli! Ani garah po! Ani lo yechola—* [Why did you bring her there? Did you think how I would feel? It's embarrassing. It's my place. I live here. I can't—]
SAMMY *(Simultaneously)*: *Tagidi li, at normalit? Amarti lach, hi ratsta le'echol sham! Ma echpat li eich targishi? At hamavi-cha po! At mavina et ze? Ve ma iti? Ani lo gar po?* [Tell me, are you normal? I told you, she wanted to eat there! What do I care how you feel? You're the embarrassing one here! Do you understand that? And what about me? I don't live here?]
TEWFIQ: It's okay!

(Tewfiq is on his feet now. But to Dina and Sammy's surprise, he is addressing Dina, not Sammy. Then:)

He make mistake! He just make mistake! But please. You can forgive! YOU CAN FORGIVE!

(A moment. Tewfiq's focus on Dina and surprising defense of Sammy have thrown everyone off balance.)

SAMMY: Don't do something like this again.
DINA: Ha. You don't.

(Sammy exits.)

I'm sorry, he . . .
TEWFIQ: Can we please go now?
DINA: I . . . *(Beat)* If you want.
TEWFIQ: I would like please to go.

(Dina nods. Tewfiq puts on his hat. They exit together.)

SCENE 11

*The sound of a lullaby. Lights up on Itzik, in the baby's room,
singing to the baby. Simon sits in the other room, with Avrum.
During the following, Avrum gradually falls asleep in his chair.
During this, elsewhere, Camal accompanies the song.*

ITZIK:

    A GREAT BIG HOUSE THERE IS SOMEWHERE
    THAT'S FILLED WITH SUN AND LOVELY THINGS.
    INSIDE THE HOUSE THERE IS A ROOM
    A BABY SLEEPS, A DADDY SINGS.

    THANK GOD HE IS A LUCKY MAN,
    A BUSY MAN, A HAPPY MAN.
    THANK GOD THE GIFT WAS GIVEN HIM
    TO FINISH ALL THE THINGS HE PLANS.

    I'M SORRY SON, I DON'T KNOW WHY
    THIS GIFT HAS NOT BEEN GIVEN ME.

IT MAKE NO DIFFERENCE HOW I TRY,
I END UP DRIFTING ON THE SEA.

WE FELL IN LOVE, YOUR MOM AND I.
WE MADE OUR PLANS AND STARTED LIFE
BUT NOW WE FIGHT AND BACK AWAY,
THE LOSER AND THE LOSER'S WIFE.

(In his own space, Camal plays and sings along.)

ITZIK:

I GUESS I AM A PATIENT MAN,
I GUESS I HAVE THE GIFT TO BE.
A QUIET ROOM, A SLEEPING CHILD,
YOU NEED THIS GIFT IF YOU'RE
   LIKE ME.

A GREAT BIG HOUSE THERE IS
   SOMEWHERE
THAT'S FULL OF SUN AND LOVELY
   THINGS.
INSIDE THE HOUSE THERE IS A
   ROOM—
A BABY SLEEPS, A DADDY SINGS.

CAMAL:

YA LEYL YA LEYLIA
TA'ALA ILAYA
YA HABIBI
YA LEYL

(Simon steps into the room.)

SIMON: I go to sleep now. I'm sorry if we cause trouble.
ITZIK: Oh, no no no, it's not you. All the time it's like this now.
   We fight, she go. It was not always like this, but now . . .
   (A moment) You know, maybe this how your concerto end.
   Not a big end, with trumpet and violin. But just like this.
   A small room. A lamp, a bed. A child sleep. And . . .

*(A moment. Then they hear the front door. Iris has returned
to the apartment. Itzik goes out into the other room, leaving
Simon with the baby.)*

Hi.

IRIS: Hi.

(*Iris prepares herself to say something very difficult. Itzik prepares to hear it. Then:*)

Itzik . . .

(*In the other room, the baby starts to cry. But Simon is alone in there, so:*)

SIMON (*Uncertain what to do*): Uhhhh . . .

(*Iris hears this*)

IRIS: *Im mi ha tinok?* [Who's with the baby?]
ITZIK (*Miming the clarinet*): The . . . man who plays the—
IRIS: *Hisha'rta otoh eem mishu zar?* [You left our baby alone with a stranger?]
ITZIK: He's not a stranger, he's—
IRIS: Idiot!

(*Iris pushes past Itzik into the other room . . . where Simon has just begun to play his concerto on his clarinet. Itzik joins her in the doorway and the two of them watch as Simon plays through to the point where his music usually cuts off . . . and then continues, completing his concerto overture for the first time. It's enough to calm the baby, who is quiet again. Then Simon sees them standing there.*)

SIMON: He was cry. I didn't know . . .
IRIS: It's okay. You . . . calm him. Thank you.

(*A moment. Then Iris starts sobbing. She cries with surprising violence. Itzik goes to comfort her, to put his arm around her. At first she instinctively pushes him away . . . but then she allows him to put his arms around her. He holds her as she cries. At last:*)

(*To Simon*) Excuse me. Excuse me.

SIMON *("I get it.")*: I am married twenty years.

AVRUM: Emm . . . *(Beat)* So I go home now. *(Beat)* If you are okay?

IRIS: *Ken, Aba.* [Yes, Dad.]

AVRUM: Okay. Very nice meet you.

SIMON: Yes. You too.

AVRUM: *Shalom aleichem.*

SIMON: *Alaikum salaam.*

> *(Avrum goes. Simon sits. Itzik and Iris sit, near their child. Transition . . .)*

SCENE 12

Lights up on the pay phone. Telephone Guy is still waiting here,
exhausted, seated against the wall. The phone rings. Before Tele-
phone Guy can react, Camal steps into view and answers it.

CAMAL: *Alloo? Aywa, ma'ak Camal.* [Hello? Yes, this is Camal.]

(The Telephone Guy deflates, shaking his head, paces.)

Aywa, min el-firqa el-musiqiyah el-masriyah . . . Aywa. Aywa,
bes . . . Ana fahimt, bes . . . Okee. Okee. [Yes of the Alexandria Ceremonial Pol . . . Yes. Yes, but . . . I understand but . . .
Okay. Okay.]

(A moment. Camal hangs up the phone. The Telephone Guy
picks up the phone again to make sure it's working and then
hangs up again.)

They will not call back.

(Camal exits. Then Dina and Tewfiq return, passing by again.)

DINA: Did she call?

TELEPHONE GUY: Not yet Dina. Soon! Soon!

(Dina and Tewfiq proceed to Dina's door. Dina reaches the door, then turns back.)

DINA: You know, Tewfiq. These songs, these movies, that we talk about before. Sometimes they are not so happy. There is love, yes. And I think that now, this night, we could live this love again. Big love, in big Arabic words. *(Arabic) Habee-bee, ana bahibak. Hal tuhibnee?* [Darling, I love you. Do you love me?] But I'm afraid I would fuck it all up. Like everything else. My life, Arab movie. Arab song.

(A silence. Then:)

TEWFIQ: Dina. My wife . . . she died because of me. We had a son. A bright and beautiful son, he made some mistakes. I was hard with him. I didn't understand. He was gentle, fragile, like her. I didn't understand him. He took his life. It broke her heart. *(Long pause)* Do you have children, Dina?

DINA: No. When I could, I was . . . occupied with nonsense. Then, when I wanted to, I couldn't.

TEWFIQ: Too bad. You are a good woman.

DINA: You think so?

TEWFIQ: I know it.

(A moment. Then Haled approaches.)

HALED: I looked on the city.

(Dina, Haled and Tewfiq all go inside together. The Telephone Guy remains visible outside, at the pay phone.)

Scene 13

Dina, Haled and Tewfiq sit in Dina's place, as before. A silence. Then:

TEWFIQ *(To Haled)*: I like Chet Baker.

(Haled is surprised. Then:)

I have all his recordings. From the beginning, with the Harry Babasin Octet to the last concert in '88.

(A moment. Then Haled pulls out his trumpet. He plays the first few sections of "My Funny Valentine." When he stops playing, Tewfiq nods approvingly. But the music continues from elsewhere, underscoring the following:)

(Standing) I will go to sleep now.

DINA: Oh. *(Then, crossing to the fridge)* You don't want some wine? I have some, in the fridge—

TEWFIQ: No. Not tonight. Not for me. It's too late.

71

DINA: Oh. Okay.

(Dina stops, uncertain what to do. Tewfiq turns to Haled.)

TEWFIQ: Don't stay up too late. We have long day tomorrow. Good night, my boy.

(Haled is surprised by the kindness. Then nods, respectfully.)

HALED: Good night, sir.
TEWFIQ: Madam.

(Tewfiq leaves Haled and Dina alone but remains visible in the hallway as Haled watches Dina, as she stares off after Tewfiq, not knowing what she's thinking.)

DINA:

IS IT A HYMN? IS IT A LOVE SONG?
THE MUSIC IS SO BEAUTIFUL,
IT MELTS AWAY SO QUICKLY

AND YOU'RE STANDING IN THE SILENCE,
STANDING IN THE DARKNESS
SINGING ABOUT WISHING.

EVERY DAY YOU STARE TO THE WEST, TO THE SOUTH—
YOU CAN SEE FOR MILES BUT IT ALL STAYS THE SAME,
THEN HONEY IN YOUR EARS, SPICE IN YOUR MOUTH . . .

HALED: You have beautiful eyes.

(Hearing this, Tewfiq exits. Then, Dina turns to Haled, steps into him, to kiss him, and . . . blackout. And the music under all this flows into . . .)

SCENE 14

Lights remain on the Telephone Guy, still waiting by the phone.
The Band Members play from the shadows.

TELEPHONE GUY:
> HERE I AM. HERE I AM.
> AND THE LIGHT IS DYING—
> WHERE ARE YOU? WHERE ARE YOU?
> WILL YOU ANSWER ME?
>
> ALL ALONE IN THE QUIET.
> AH, MY EARS ARE THIRSTY
> FOR YOUR VOICE, FOR YOUR VOICE.
> CAN YOU ANSWER ME?
>
> IF I TRY MAYBE I CAN SEE YOUR SHADOW
> IN THE SODIUM LIGHT THAT MASQUERADES AS MOON.
> IF I TRY, I MIGHT TAKE OFF LIKE A SPARROW
> AND I'LL TRAVEL ALONG A GUIDING BREEZE . . .
> "VERY SOON, VERY SOON."

THAT'S THE SOUND OF LONGING.
ARE YOU THERE? ARE YOU THERE?
WILL YOU ANSWER ME?

(The Telephone Guy walks away from the phone, having given up at last. Then the pay phone rings. The Telephone Guy rushes back to it, eagerly, and answers. From the shadows, Camal sees this.)

Alo? Amalia, zot at? Ma shlomech? Ani? Beseder! Ani lovesh et ha sveder she saragt li. Ze mechamem oti. [Hello? Amalia, is that you? How are you? Me? I'm fine, I'm fine! I'm wearing the sweater you made me. It keeps me warm.]

(As Telephone Guy speaks, we see his words translated, projected on the wall above him. And then we begin to see the rest of our characters, wherever they all are, alone.)

SAMMY:

IN MY DREAMS MY BELOVED LIES BESIDE ME—

SAMMY/ZELGER:

WHEN THE SUN LIGHTS THE ROOM I FIND IT'S ONLY
ME.

CAMAL:

ONLY ME—

ANNA:

ONLY YOU WHEN THE SUN IS GONE—

AVRUM:

ONLY ME—

PAPI:

ONLY ME WHEN THE MOON IS—

JULIA/SIMON:
    WITH THE WORLD AROUND ME.
ANNA/SAMMY/CAMAL/ITZIK:
    WITH THE WORLD AROUND ME.
    AHH—
IRIS/DINA/PAPI/HALED:
    WITH THE WORLD AROUND YOU—
    AHH

SIMON/ZELGER/JULIA/AVRUM:
    WITH THE WORLD AROUND,
    AHH—

ITZIK:
    WITH THE WORLD—
IRIS:
    ALL AROUND ME—

TELEPHONE GUY:
    ONLY YOU,
    WHEN THE SUN AND MOON
    AND STARS ARE GONE,
    WHAT'S LEFT IS ONLY YOU.

EVERYONE:
    WILL YOU ANSWER ME?
    ANSWER ME.

    (*And we transition to . . .*)

SCENE 15

Morning, outside Dina's café. Papi emerges, opening the café as before. Itzik approaches. Dina emerges and approaches the café. And during this the Band gathers as well, dragging their suitcases. Tewfiq greets Simon. Haled emerges, not looking at Dina. When all are gathered, Tewfiq approaches Dina. He removes his hat.

TEWFIQ: Madam. On behalf of the Alexandria Ceremonial Police Orchestra, I would like to thank you for your hospitality. We shall be ever grateful.
DINA: My pleasure.

(Tewfiq puts his hat back on and turns to go.)

Tewfiq.

(Tewfiq turns back. She hands him a slip of paper.)

This is the place. *Petah Tikvah.*

(Tewfiq nods and starts to slip the paper into his jacket. Then, with great emotion:)

TEWFIQ: Goodbye, madam.

(Tewfiq walks toward the Band, now neatly lined up. He turns back and waves to Dina. Dina waves back. The Band is gone . . . Papi and Itzik are gone . . . The town is gone. Back into mirage . . .)

DINA: Once, not long ago, a group of musicians came to Israel, from Egypt.

(. . . And now the Band begins to appear again, to line up, for their concert . . .)

You probably didn't hear about it. It wasn't very important.

(. . . Dina is gone. Tewfiq stands before his Band. He faces the audience. Then turns to face his Musicians. And as the music swells, Tewfiq raises his hands, suspends them . . . The music suspends at its peak . . . And Tewfiq drops his hands.
  Blackout.)

THE END

(Or is it? Because after the curtain call, the Band plays a rousing number to send us home . . .)